ice cream

ice cream

sorbets, frozen yogurts, parfaits, bombes, and more

shona crawford poole

photography by william lingwood

conran
OCTOPUS

INTRODUCTION

Real ices made with ripe fruit, fresh dairy cream, and natural flavours are a startling improvement on what most mass manufacturers call ice cream. The stuff they make with all those nameless fats, unpronounceable emulsifiers, numbered flavorings, and coded colors is edible, but it is not the stuff of frozen dreams. Much more appealing are the luxury ice cream ranges made with real dairy ingredients, but they are often sweetly bland.

In the finest restaurants, chefs make sorbets daily. This is not because they cannot make a sufficient quantity at once to last for a week or two, but rather because ices, particularly fruit ices, taste best when freshly made. For many cooks this is a counsel of perfection that will take second place to the convenience of having iced puddings on tap. But it is worth noticing the difference freshness makes to taste and that longer storage makes to texture.

Freezing in an ice cream maker
Sooner or later, serious ice cream fanciers will want an ice cream maker, sometimes called a *sorbetière*. There are two basic types of electric ice cream maker that churn and freeze simultaneously.

The larger, and more expensive, machines, have their own refrigeration unit, and work independently. Their big advantage is their ability to work continuously and make one batch after another. Most freeze about 1¾ pints (1 liter) at a time and take about 30 minutes, though timings are influenced by the mix of ingredients and the temperature of the day. Models with a freezer bowl that can be removed for washing have an obvious practical advantage.

Less expensive, and just as quick to use, are ice cream makers based on a cold-retaining bowl. The detachable bowl has to be frozen for about 24 hours in the freezer before it is fitted into the ice cream machine, which then churns and freezes the ice.

These machines take up less space on the kitchen worktop and are lighter to lift. They are usually large enough to make up to 1¾ pints (1 liter) of ice cream, but they cannot make more than a single batch at any one time.

An old-fashioned, hand-cranked churn requiring the addition of ice, salt, and human motor power makes ices that are every bit as smooth as those produced in an electric ice cream maker.

Freshly churned and frozen ice cream can be served at once, or transferred to a chilled container, covered, and put in the freezer until needed. Many of the sorbets and custard-based ices are quite soft when newly made and will be the better for an hour or so in the freezer before serving.

Still-freezing

Still-freezing involves freezing without simultaneously stirring or churning. It simply involves using a flat-bottomed container for the ice cream mixture and putting it in the freezer until it is firm. Most ice creams and sorbets need whisking or beating during freezing to break up the ice crystals and make the frozen mixture pleasantly smooth.

As a general rule, the richer or sweeter the recipe, the less stirring or whisking it will need. Large flakes or crystals of ice form most readily in the least sweet or creamy ices, which must be taken out of the freezer and beaten to reduce the size of the ice crystals, at least once during the freezing process.

The best possible time to beat any ice that does require whisking while it freezes is when the mixture at the sides and bottom of the container is almost firm and the center is fairly liquid. The partly frozen mixture should be tipped into a chilled bowl and beaten vigorously. This can also be done in a food processor, but it does not achieve quite the same aerating effect as a well-timed beating. The whisked ice is then returned to the freezer to firm again. An overlooked ice that has frozen hard before beating is better softened in the refrigerator than at room temperature.

There are also plenty of ices in this book that can be frozen without any stirring at all. Most of these are simple to make too, and most of them are either fairly rich, or sweet, or both. This is because sugar and fat are two ingredients that, like alcohol, inhibit the formation of large, gritty ice crystals.

When still-freezing, remember that the colder the temperature, the faster the mixture will freeze, and the smaller the crystals of ice formed in it will be. Choose flat rather than deep containers and the coldest part of the freezer.

Freezing times are so variable that even the vaguest instructions can be more misleading than helpful. Obviously, a modern freezer working on its fast-freeze setting will do the job much more efficiently than the ice-making compartment of a small, old refrigerator in a warm kitchen.

Ripening ices

After a day or two stored in the freezer, most ices will be rock-hard and will require ripening to show themselves at their best. Ripening or softening to the consistency that makes the most of its flavor and texture should always be done slowly in the refrigerator. The aim is to soften it enough to scoop and serve, or simply eat, and, as with freezing, timing will depend on a number of factors.

Small quantities, individual servings, or ices in flat containers will ripen more quickly than ices in deep containers or bombe molds. Small ices will probably need only 5 or 10 minutes. Bombes or big containers, 30 minutes or so.

The sweetest and most alcoholic ices will tend to ripen fastest, and those from the coldest freezers will take longest to ripen.

Ingredients

Cream, a key ingredient in ice cream, varies in fat content and description. In Britain, single cream contains about 18 percent fat, whipping cream 35 percent and double cream 48 percent. Clotted cream is thicker and richer still with a fat content of 55–60 percent. American half-and-half cream is lighter than single cream, containing 10–12 percent fat, and US medium cream contains 25 percent fat. Most fresh cream sold is pasteurized. Untreated cream, usually from Guernsey or Jersey cows, and organically produced cream (which may or may not be pasteurized), can have richer and more interesting flavors than the standard products.

Large eggs have been used throughout this book. The possibility that some eggs may contain salmonella bacteria, one of the commonest causes of food poisoning, has given rise to the advice that recipes containing raw egg should not be eaten by pregnant women, babies, frail, elderly people, or anyone whose immune system is compromised. Salmonella bacteria are killed by heating to 160°F/70°C and being held at that temperature for two minutes.

Flavorings may be natural or synthetic and, not surprisingly, natural flavors usually have more complexity and charm than their laboratory-produced imitators. The word "extract" usually implies a natural flavor, and "essence" and "flavoring" an artificial one. The strength of either type can vary widely although, as a general rule, natural extracts can be used by the teaspoon, and artificial essences by the drop.

I like to cook with organically produced ingredients, so, wherever possible, the recipes in this book have been tested using them. Taste is subjective of course, but I believe that organic produce has more flavor and I enjoy the idea that it is produced by sustainable agricultural methods and without synthetic chemicals or genetically modified species. It is true that part of the satisfaction of using organics is aesthetic, and why not? Why make ice creams and sorbets for anything but pleasure?

Transforming fresh fruit and low-fat dairy produce into memorably good ice creams and sorbets is quicker and easier than it has ever been. An electric juicer takes the sweat out of liquidizing and sieving fruit. And an electric ice cream maker beats while it freezes, ensuring that every ice turns out silky smooth, even when there is little fat or sugar to help keep down the size of the ice crystals. So here is a starter kit of mix-and-match recipes to show you that taste does not have to be sacrificed for the sake of HEALTH

Fromage frais is a fresh-tasting, low-calorie alternative to cream in ices. To make jazzy ice lollipops, freeze the lemon grass ice cream mixture in ice lollipop molds using sticks of lemon grass, thick end in the ice, for handles.

SERVES 6

5oz/150g granulated sugar
2 sticks of lemon grass, finely sliced
juice of 1 lemon
9oz/250g creamy fromage frais

To serve
6 or more sticks of lemon grass (optional)

Add ½ pint/300ml water to the sugar and sliced lemon grass in a small pan. Heat slowly until the sugar has dissolved completely, then simmer for 1 minute, take off the heat, and set aside until cold.

Strain the lemon grass syrup into a bowl and whisk in the lemon juice and fromage frais.

Freeze in an ice cream maker, following the manufacturer's instructions. Or still-freeze (page 8), whisking the partially frozen ice at least once during the freezing process.

To make ice lollipops, chill the molds. Freeze the ice cream mixture until it is a firm-enough slush to support the lollipop sticks in position. Fill the chilled molds, pop in the sticks, and freeze until very firm.

Traditionally, ricotta is a smooth and slightly sweet fresh cheese made from the ewes' milk whey, though cows' milk ricotta is probably more widely available now. Ricotta that is enriched with whole milk loses its useful low-fat status. Serve vanilla ricotta gelato with sugared or marinated summer and fall berries.

SERVES 6

1lb/450g very fresh ricotta
4 egg yolks
5 oz/150g caster sugar
real vanilla extract, to taste

To ensure that the ice is as smooth as possible, push the ricotta through a fine sieve or blend it in a food processor.

Combine the egg yolks and sugar in a bowl and whisk until the mixture is very pale and thick. Whisk in the smooth ricotta and 2 teaspoons of vanilla extract. Taste and add more vanilla extract if needed, bearing in mind that flavor fades with freezing.

Freeze in an ice cream maker, following the manufacturer's instructions. Or still-freeze (page 8), whisking the partially frozen ice at least once during the freezing process.

LEMON GRASS &
FROMAGE FRAIS ICE CREAM

LIME & PAPAYA CRUSH

Papayas, called paw paws in many parts of the world, can be as small as an apple, and as large as a football. Whatever its dimensions, a good papaya has dense, highly perfumed flesh that has a real affinity with lime and also makes a silky sorbet.

SERVES 6

2lb/1kg ripe papayas
1 lime, preferably unwaxed
5oz/150g caster sugar

Halve the papayas and scoop out and discard the seeds. Spoon the flesh into a blender or processor, discarding the skin. Blend or process the flesh to a smooth purée, and, ideally, sieve it.

Wash and dry the lime. Take off the zest using a fine grater. Squeeze and strain the juice.

Combine the papaya purée with the lime juice and zest, add the sugar and stir until it has dissolved. To allow the flavor to develop, and if you have time, chill the papaya purée for 1–2 hours in the refrigerator before freezing.

Freeze in an ice cream maker, following the manufacturer's instructions. Or still-freeze (page 8), whisking the partially frozen ice at least once during the freezing process.

Peaches are one of those maddening summer fruits that are not worth eating until they are fully ripe and heavy with juice. Equally maddening, they all ripen together and once ripe demand to be eaten immediately because they won't keep. Freeze the glut in this luxuriously profligate ice.

SERVES 6

2lb/1kg fully ripe peaches
2 tablespoons fresh lemon juice
7oz/200g caster sugar

Peel and stone the peaches, and juice the flesh. Alternatively, liquidize or process the flesh and pass it through a sieve. Stir in the lemon juice and sugar. Chill the mixture for an hour or more in the refrigerator, stirring it from time to time to dissolve the sugar completely and to allow the flavor to develop.

Freeze in an ice cream maker, following the manufacturer's instructions. Or still-freeze (page 8), whisking the partially frozen ice at least once during the freezing process.

Variation

NECTARINE FREEZE The peach's smooth-skinned sister, the nectarine, usually has more acidity, so orange juice can be substituted for lemon juice.

Flavor natural yogurt with the deep, rich taste of real maple syrup and stir in chopped pecans for a deliciously simple ice. The richer the yogurt, the easier it is to make a smooth-textured ice. Thick, Greek-style yogurt gives the best results of all.

SERVES 6

6 to 8 tablespoons maple syrup
18fl oz/500ml natural yogurt
4oz/120g freshly shelled pecan nuts,
    chopped

Stir 6 tablespoons of maple syrup into the yogurt. Taste and add more maple syrup if the mixture is not sweet enough.

Freeze in an ice cream maker, following the manufacturer's instructions. Or still-freeze (page 8), whisking the partially frozen ice at least once during the freezing process.

Finally, stir the chopped pecans into the thickened ice cream before freezing it until firm.

Caramelized honey has a flavor that is almost familiar and oddly fascinating. Combine it with a hint of cinnamon and some creamy yogurt to make a luxurious ice that's also nice and light.

SERVES 6

7oz/200g honey
½ teaspoon freshly ground cinnamon
1 pint/600ml creamy, natural yogurt

If the honey is thick, stand the jar up to its neck in hot water until it melts enough to pour. Pour 7oz/200g into a pan, bring it to the boil, and continue heating until it starts to caramelize. The smell will tell you when the sugars start to burn, but don't let the honey darken too much or it will taste bitter. When you judge the process has gone far enough, take the pan off the heat and stir in 6 tablespoons of cold water. Allow the honey caramel syrup to cool a little before stirring in the cinnamon, then leave it until quite cold.

Combine the cold syrup with the yogurt and mix well. Freeze in an ice cream maker, following the manufacturer's instructions. Or still-freeze (page 8), whisking the partially frozen ice at least once during the freezing process.

MAPLE & PECAN YOGURT ICE

CAROB & MASCARPONE ICE CREAM

Carob powder is a useful substitute for cocoa in recipes where the taste of chocolate is wanted, but without the side effects experienced by some migraine sufferers and others sensitive to substances in cocoa. Carob powder is available in health food shops. Note that carob confectionery bars are not a satisfactory substitute for carob powder, but any other rich, fresh cream cheese can be substituted for Italian mascarpone.

SERVES 6

4 egg yolks
6oz/175g soft, light brown sugar
4 tablespoons carob powder
½ pint/300ml milk
9oz/250g mascarpone
real vanilla extract, to taste

Whisk the egg yolks with the sugar until the mixture is pale and fluffy, then whisk in the carob powder. Gradually whisk in the milk.

Cook this custard mixture, heating it gently in a heavy pan over a very low heat, or cook it in the top of a double boiler, stirring constantly until the custard is thick enough to coat the back of a wooden spoon. Do not let it boil.

Remove the custard from the heat, cover, and set aside to cool.

Whisk the cold carob custard into the mascarpone before adding vanilla extract to taste. Remember that flavor fades when a mixture is frozen.

Freeze in an ice cream maker, following the manufacturer's instructions. Or still-freeze (page 8), whisking the partially frozen ice at least once during the freezing process.

Variations

CHOCOLATE AND MASCARPONE ICE CREAM Swap top-quality cocoa for the carob powder. Chocolate extract can be substituted for the vanilla extract.

MOCHA MASCARPONE ICE CREAM Make the custard without extra flavoring, and add 4 tablespoons of strong espresso coffee instead of the vanilla to the cold custard. Add a little more coffee for a more strongly flavored ice.

This is tart, refreshing, and not too sweet. It can be served as a light first course on a hot summer's day.

SERVES 6

3 large pink grapefruit
6oz/175g granulated sugar
4 tablespoons chopped fresh mint

Cut the zest from one of the grapefruit using a very sharp knife or vegetable peeler, taking care not to include any of the pith.

Pour ½ pint/300ml water into a pan and add the zest and sugar. Heat gently until the sugar has dissolved completely. Simmer the syrup for 5 minutes, then take it off the heat, and stir in the mint. Set it aside until quite cold.

Squeeze the juice from all the grapefruit and strain it. Strain the cold syrup and stir it into the grapefruit juice.

Freeze in an ice cream maker, following the manufacturer's instructions. Or still-freeze (page 8), whisking the partially frozen ice at least once during the freezing process.

More chopped mint can be stirred into the partially frozen sorbet for a pretty effect and a mintier taste.

PINK GRAPEFRUIT & MINT SORBET

GOOSEBERRY & ELDERFLOWER SORBET

Even city folk can find elderflowers in municipal parks in early summer when the first green gooseberries appear. Together they make a sorbet that has something of the lovely perfume of muscat grapes. Dried elderflowers, sold by herbalists, can be used instead of fresh blossom, or elderflower cordial substituted for a proportion of the water; the amount will depend on the cordial's strength.

SERVES 6

2lb/900g green (cooking) gooseberries
8oz/225g granulated sugar
about 3 large elderflower heads

Wash the gooseberries (there is no need to top and tail them) and put them, whole, into a saucepan with 1 pint/600ml water. Simmer the fruit until it is tender, then strain the juice through a scalded jelly bag, or through a large sieve lined with a clean cloth. Knot the corners of the cloth and hang it up until it stops dripping.

Tie the elderflower heads loosely in a piece of muslin (cheesecloth) and put them into a pan with the gooseberry juice and the sugar. Heat gently until the sugar has dissolved completely, bring to the boil, then cool immediately. By the time the syrup is quite cold, the elderflowers will have perfumed it strongly.

Discard the elderflowers and freeze the syrup in an ice cream maker, following the manufacturer's instructions. Or still-freeze (page 8), whisking the partially frozen mixture at least twice during the freezing process.

PINK GRAPEFRUIT & MINT SORBET

PRUNE ICE CREAM

Liberate the long-suffering prune from its 'custard and sniggers', English schoolboy image by transforming it into this gorgeous, grown-up ice. Prune ice cream is a worthy candidate for a slosh of optional alcohol. Almost any spirit, from gin to cognac, does the trick. Use Indian or China tea at normal strength for this recipe.

SERVES 6

1lb/450g plump, ready-to-eat prunes
about 1½ pints/900ml cold tea
zest of half an orange, in long strips
4oz/120g soft, light brown sugar
½ pint/300ml whipping cream, chilled
2 tablespoons gin (optional)

Soak the prunes and the orange zest in the tea overnight. Add the sugar and simmer in a pan until tender. Set aside until the prunes are cool enough to handle.

Stone the prunes and discard the orange zest. Purée the fruit with its cooking syrup either by passing it through a sieve, or by processing it in a blender or food processor and then straining it. Stir in the gin, if used.

Whip the cream until it holds soft peaks. Combine with prune purée.

Freeze in an ice cream maker, following the manufacturer's instructions. Or still-freeze (page 8), whisking the partially frozen ice at least once during the freezing process.

Variation

Substitute dried apricots for the prunes to make deeply flavored, golden ice cream.

APPLE & RUNNY HONEY SORBET

This smooth apple sorbet is peachy-pink and intensely flavored. Beware of overpowering the apple taste with a too highly scented honey. A hint of honey is lovely. Choose apples of character—whether for eating or cooking: McIntosh or Granny Smith apples are good.

SERVES 6

2 pints/1.2 liters unsweetened apple juice
1½ lb/700g apples
6oz/175g granulated sugar
2 tablespoons clear honey

Bring the apple juice to the boil in a heavy pan and simmer, uncovered, until reduced to about 1 pint/600ml.

Peel, core, and roughly chop the apples. Add the apples and sugar to the juice and cook gently until the apples are tender. Stir in the honey and set aside to cool.

Blend or process the apples to a smooth purée, or pass through a fine sieve.

Freeze in an ice cream maker, following the manufacturer's instructions. Or still-freeze (page 8), whisking the partially frozen ice at least once during the freezing process.

The contrast of ginger heat with icy fruit juice makes a taste treat that feels like a tonic.

SERVES 6

1 ripe pineapple (about 2 lb/1kg)
1in/2.5cm cube peeled fresh ginger,
    chopped
juice of 1 lemon or lime
5oz/150g caster sugar

Top and tail the pineapple, then slice it vertically into wedges. Cut off the skin as economically as possible, removing all the dark "eyes", before chopping the flesh into large chunks.

Juice the pineapple chunks with the ginger in an electric juicer, stir in the lemon or lime juice, and measure the liquid. Alternatively, blend or process the pineapple, ginger, and lemon or lime juice, then strain and measure the liquid. Add cold water if any is needed to bring the volume up to 1 pint/600ml.

Combine the pineapple juice with the sugar and stir until it has dissolved. To allow the flavor to develop, and if you have time, chill the mixture for 1–2 hours in the refrigerator before freezing.

Freeze in an ice cream maker, following the manufacturer's instructions. Or still-freeze (page 8), whisking the partially frozen ice at least once during the freezing process.

Photograph on pages 10–11

Variations

PINEAPPLE & TWO GINGERS SORBET Halve the quantity of fresh ginger and add four tablespoons of finely chopped preserved ginger to the freshly frozen ice. Either candied ginger or ginger preserved in syrup is fine.

MELON & FRESH GINGER SORBET Use a powerfully fragrant melon in place of the pineapple, and go easy on the ginger—just a hint will do here.

Who says ice cream is for kids? Think cocktails, then think desserts. These ices are pretty grown-up stuff, sparkling sorbets and creamy set pieces for elegant dinners or special occasions. And practice makes perfect, which is a great excuse for making muscat sorbet or zabaglione semifreddo to enjoy on a quiet evening at home. Wine sorbets are best eaten on the day they are made, but creamy liqueur parfaits will be none the worse for several days in the freezer—if you can resist them for that long. Choose from these recipes to give your meal a touch of unforgettable SOPHISTICATION

Granitas are intentionally crunchy ices. An occasional, desultory stir—and no beating—during freezing is all that is required to produce the flaky crystals of ice that are their hallmark. Raspberries have an affinity with red wine that is shown to great advantage in this ice.

SERVES 6

4oz/120g fresh or frozen raspberries, thawed if frozen
6oz/175g granulated sugar
1 pint/600ml red Bordeaux wine

Purée the raspberries or process in a blender or food processor, then pass the pulp through a fine sieve to remove the pips. Set the purée aside.

Pour 4fl oz/125ml water into a small pan and add the sugar. Heat gently until the sugar has dissolved completely. Raise the heat and boil the syrup for 5 minutes, then set it aside to cool. When the syrup is quite cold, combine with the raspberry purée and wine.

To still-freeze, pour the mixture into a shallow, flat-bottomed container (preferably a metal tray, but a plastic box will also do) and freeze until the edges are firm and the center of the ice is still liquid. Stir the sides to the center with a fork, then return the mixture to the freezer until not too firm.

If frozen in an ice cream maker, this recipe creates a smooth ice that is also delightful.

Zabaglione is the simplest of spectacular puddings—just egg yolks, sugar, and Marsala (for which a medium or sweet sherry may be substituted at a pinch). In its warm form, zabaglione has to be made just before it is served, so this iced version is a more practical proposition for entertaining.

SERVES 6

4 egg yolks
4oz/120g caster sugar
¼ pint/150ml dry Marsala
¼ pint/150ml whipping cream, chilled

Separate the egg yolks into a fairly large bowl that will fit over a pan. Add the sugar and whisk until the mixture is very pale and falls back leaving a trail when the beaters are lifted.

Whisk in the Marsala, then set the bowl over a pan of simmering water and continue whisking until the mixture has at least doubled its volume. Take off the heat and put the bowl in cold water, or over ice, and whisk until the mixture is cold.

Whip the cream until it holds soft peaks. Combine it with the cold zabaglione and whisk them together lightly.

Turn the mixture into small stemmed glasses or individual dishes and freeze until firm. Serve with butter tuiles (page 86).

Photograph on pages 24–25

CLARET GRANITA

CHAMPAGNE SORBET

Like champagne cocktails, champagne ices call for nothing too grand in the way of wine. Alcohol inhibits the formation of ice crystals, so this ice is unlikely to freeze rock hard at domestic freezer temperatures and should need no ripening before serving.

SERVES 6

2 juicy oranges
4oz/120g caster sugar
1 pint/600ml champagne or sparkling
    white wine
4 tablespoons brandy
¼ teaspoon Angostura or orange bitters

Cut the zest from the oranges, using a very sharp knife or vegetable peeler, taking care not to include any of the pith. Squeeze, strain, and reserve the juice.

Add the orange zest and sugar to 8 tablespoons of water in a pan and heat gently until the sugar has dissolved completely. Raise the heat and boil the syrup for 5 minutes, then set it aside to cool completely.

When the syrup is cold, discard the orange zest, and stir the orange juice, champagne, or sparkling white wine, brandy, and bitters into the cold syrup.

Freeze in an ice cream maker, following the manufacturer's instructions. Or still-freeze (page 8), whisking the partially frozen ice at least once during the freezing process.

Lemon sorbet served with a splash of iced vodka is a marriage made in heaven. This recipe goes a stage further, freezing the two together at the outset. Ices made with alcohol are never very stable, so plan to use lemon vodka sorbet within 48 hours of making it.

Organic lemons, and those labeled "unwaxed" are best in recipes like this, which use the zest. And even though they are not preserved with a coat of fungicidal wax, it is still a good idea to wash the skins.

SERVES 6

4 lemons, preferably unwaxed
7oz/200g granulated sugar
6 tablespoons vodka

Cut the zest from two of the lemons using a very sharp knife or vegetable peeler, taking care not to include any of the pith. Put the zest in a pan with the sugar and ¾ pint/450ml water and heat slowly, stirring until the sugar has dissolved completely, then simmer for 5 minutes. Set the syrup aside to infuse for several hours, preferably overnight.

Squeeze the juice from all the lemons and strain it. Strain the syrup, discarding the lemon zest, and mix it with the lemon juice. Stir in the vodka.

Freeze in an ice cream maker, following the manufacturer's instructions. Or still-freeze (page 8), whisking the partially frozen ice at least once during the freezing process.

Photograph on page 4

Wild or cultivated blueberries can be used for this unusual ice, as can hedgerow brambles or elderberries. The berries vary in acidity, so adjust the sugar to your taste. Use all wine, or a mixture of wine and water.

SERVES 6

8oz/225g blueberries
6oz/175g granulated sugar
1 pint/600ml full-bodied red wine

Pour the wine into a pan and add the blueberries and sugar. Heat, stirring, until the sugar has dissolved completely. Bring to the boil, simmer for 1 minute, and set aside until cold.

Blend or process the fruit with the wine, then sieve it.

Freeze in an ice cream maker, following the manufacturer's instructions. Or still-freeze (page 8), whisking the partially frozen ice at least once during the freezing process.

All kinds of fruits are used to flavor the strong, colorless, unsweetened spirits that are so popular in the mountainous regions of Europe. The raspberry and pear-flavored varieties are the most successful in sorbets. Perry is to pears is what cider is to apples.

SERVES 6

175g/6oz granulated sugar
½ pint/300ml perry
6 tablespoons *Poire Williams eau-de-vie*
2 tablespoons lemon juice

Add the sugar to the perry and ½ pint/300ml water in a pan and heat gently until the sugar has dissolved completely. Raise the heat and boil the syrup for 5 minutes. Set aside until cold, then stir in the *Poire Williams eau-de-vie* and lemon juice.

Freeze in an ice cream maker, following the manufacturer's instructions. Or still-freeze (page 8), whisking the partially frozen ice at least once during the freezing process.

Variation

APPLE & CIDER BRANDY SORBET Good, single-variety Somerset cider can be very dry, but, like its distilled stablemate, cider apple brandy, it is packed with concentrated apple flavor. Use cider and cider apple brandy in place of the perry and *eau de vie*, adjusting the sweetness to take account of the ingredients and your taste.

BLUEBERRY & RED WINE SORBET

Throughout the Caribbean islands, dark rum, fresh lime juice, and sugar are the backbone of rum punch. For variations, add and subtract fresh pineapple, oranges, coconut milk, bitters, and scarlet grenadine syrup, which is made from the juice of pomegranates.

SERVES 6

juice of 4 limes

¼ pint/150ml fresh pineapple juice or
    orange juice

8oz/225g sugar

8 tablespoons dark rum

2 tablespoons grenadine syrup

¼ teaspoon Angostura or orange bitters

Combine the lime juice and pineapple or orange juice with the sugar and enough cold water to make up ¾ pint/425ml. Stir until the sugar has dissolved completely, then add the rum, grenadine syrup, and bitters.

Freeze in an ice cream maker, following the manufacturer's instructions. Or still-freeze (page 8), whisking the partially frozen ice at least once during the freezing process.

FROZEN RUM PUNCH

MUSCAT SORBET

Dessert wines based on sweet, fragrant muscat grapes make lovely sorbets.

SERVES 6

4oz/120g granulated sugar

juice of 1 lemon

1 pint/600ml muscat dessert wine

Measure 8 tablespoons of water into a pan and add the sugar. Heat gently until the sugar has dissolved completely. Raise the heat and boil the syrup for 5 minutes, then set it aside to cool.

When it is cold, stir in the lemon juice and wine.

Freeze in an ice cream maker, following the manufacturer's instructions. Or still-freeze (page 8), whisking the partially frozen ice at least once during the freezing process.

Parfaits are rich, smooth ices. They are often flavored with liqueurs and frozen in individual, freezer-proof serving dishes. Stemmed, colored glasses also make pretty containers. Or the rims of plain glasses can be frosted with plain or colored sugar. For orange sugar frosting to go with a Cointreau or Grand Marnier parfait, dip the rims of the glasses first in undiluted orange squash and then immediately into granulated sugar. Chill until needed. If you are using tall glasses, check that they have room to stand in the freezer.

SERVES 6

8oz/225g granulated sugar
4 egg yolks
4 tablespoons liqueur
2 egg whites
8fl oz /225ml whipping cream, chilled

Measure 6 tablespoons of water into a small, heavy pan and add the sugar. Heat gently, stirring, until the sugar has dissolved completely. Wash down any sugar crystals from the sides of the pan with a pastry brush dipped in cold water, then raise the heat and boil the syrup until it is just beginning to color (about 300°F/150°C on a sugar thermometer). Take the pan off the heat and set it aside to cool for 1 minute.

Add the egg yolks to a large bowl and whisk in the hot syrup, and continue whisking until the mixture is cool and has tripled its original volume. Whisk in the liqueur, then chill the mixture in the refrigerator.

Whisk the egg whites until they hold stiff peaks. Whip the cream until it holds soft peaks. Combine the yolk mixture with the whisked egg whites and cream, and whisk them lightly together. Turn the parfait into individual dishes, cover, and freeze until firm.

Port needs no additional sugar to make a superb luxurious and alcoholic ice. This is a dense ice, but it does not freeze hard, so can be served straight from the freezer without ripening in the refrigerator.

SERVES 6

½ pint/300ml fresh orange juice
¾ pint/425ml port

Strain the orange juice and combine it with the port.

Freeze in an ice cream maker, following the manufacturer's instructions. Or still-freeze (page 8), whisking the partially frozen ice at least once during the freezing process.

Take milk, cream, eggs, and butter from the fridge and flavor them with

sugar, spice, nuts, and chocolate from the store-cupboard in endlessly

inventive combinations. These classic recipes taste so good that it is easy to

overlook their sound nutritional value. Choose between the smooth, crisp

texture of vanilla ice cream made with egg yolks and milk, and richer ices

such as chocolate or butterscotch that include cream and butter. What to do

with the leftover egg whites? Think crisp and crunchy—meringues, ratafias, and

tuiles to serve with these heavenly homemade CLASSIC ICES

VANILLA ICE CREAM WITH CHOCOLATE CHIPS

This recipe is for a classic vanilla ice cream based on a custard made with egg yolks and milk. It is dense, sweet, and crisp. The quantity of sugar may be reduced by as much as half, and skimmed or semiskimmed milk substituted for whole milk. The result will obviously be less rich and it will be best eaten when it is freshly churned.

Egg custards thicken below boiling point, and must not boil or they will curdle. It is a safe bet to cook them in a double boiler, or a bowl over simmering water.

SERVES 6

1 vanilla pod, or real vanilla extract, to taste
1¼ pints/750ml whole milk
6 egg yolks
9oz/275g caster sugar
a pinch of salt

If using a vanilla pod, halve it lengthways and put it into a heavy pan with the milk. Heat gently to near-boiling point, then remove from the heat, and set it aside for 30 minutes to infuse. If using vanilla extract, there is no need to heat the milk. Add vanilla extract to taste when the custard has cooled.

Combine the egg yolks, sugar, and salt in a bowl. Whisk until the mixture is very pale and falls back leaving a trail when the beaters are lifted. Remove the vanilla pod from the milk and gradually whisk the milk into the egg mixture.

Cook the custard in a heavy-based pan over a very low heat, or in the top of a double boiler, stirring constantly until thickened enough to coat the back of a wooden spoon.

Remove the custard from the heat, cover, and set it aside to cool. Vanilla extract should be added at this point, remembering that the flavor will fade with freezing.

Freeze in an ice cream maker, following the manufacturer's instructions. Or still-freeze (page 8), whisking the partially frozen ice at least once during the freezing process.

Variations

Real, old-fashioned vanilla ice cream made with an egg custard is the basis of many more perennial favorites.

CHOCOLATE CHIP ICE CREAM Coarsely grate 3½oz/100g good-quality chocolate, milk or plain, and stir it into vanilla ice cream that is frozen but is not yet quite firm.

CASSATA ICE CREAM Stir 3½oz/100g of mixed, chopped, dried, and candied fruits into vanilla ice cream that has been frozen but is not yet quite firm.

RUM & RAISIN ICE CREAM Soak 3oz/85g raisins in 4 tablespoons of rum or a rum-flavored syrup until they are plump and stir them into vanilla ice cream that has been frozen but is not yet quite firm.

Nut ices made commercially are rarely as appealing as those made at home. Hazelnuts, almonds, walnuts, and pistachio nuts all make excellent ice creams. They can be added to the vanilla ice cream recipe (page 37), omitting the vanilla flavouring, or you can try this richer recipe.

SERVES 6

4oz/120g shelled hazelnuts
4 egg yolks
6oz/175g caster sugar
½ pint/300ml milk
½ pint/300ml whipping cream, chilled

Heat the oven to 325°F/160°C/gas 3.

Spread the hazelnuts on a baking sheet and toast them in the oven for 10 to 15 minutes, or until their centers turn a pale beige colour. Turn the nuts onto a cloth, let them cool, and rub off the skins. Chop the nuts finely in a food processor or electric coffee mill. Set aside.

Combine the egg yolks and sugar in a bowl. Whisk until the mixture is very pale and falls back leaving a trail when the beaters are lifted. Gradually beat in the milk.

Cook the custard carefully in a heavy saucepan over a low heat, or in the top of a double boiler, stirring constantly until it is thick enough to coat the back of a wooden spoon. Take the custard off the heat, cover, and set it aside to cool.

Stir the ground hazelnuts into the cold custard. Whip the cream until it holds soft peaks and fold it in.

Freeze in an ice cream maker, following the manufacturer's instructions. Or still-freeze (page 8), whisking the partially frozen ice at least once during the freezing process.

Variations

ALMOND ICE CREAM Substitute blanched almonds for the hazelnuts and add a few drops of almond essence.

WALNUT ICE CREAM Use freshly shelled walnuts and a tablespoon or two of medium or sweet sherry. There is no need to toast the nuts.

PISTACHIO ICE CREAM Shelled pistachios do not need toasting before adding to the custard. Add a little almond essence too. A drop or two of green food coloring is an old-fashioned addition.

HAZELNUT ICE CREAM

HAZELNUT ICE CREAM

SAFFRON & MACE ICE CREAM

A few strands of saffron are enough to infuse a whole batch of ice cream with this costly spice's earthy warmth and to color it bright yellow. Mace, the outside husk of nutmeg, is another warm spice. If mace is not available, use freshly grated nutmeg, adding it to the cooled custard.

SERVES 6

1¼ pints/750ml whole milk
20 strands of saffron
2 blades of mace
6 egg yolks
9oz/275g caster sugar

Pour the milk into a pan and add the saffron and mace. Bring almost to the boil, then remove the pan from the heat, and leave to infuse for 1 hour or more.

Combine the egg yolks and sugar in a bowl. Whisk until the mixture is very pale and falls back leaving a trail when the beaters are lifted. Strain the milk and gradually whisk it into the egg mixture.

Cook the custard carefully in a heavy pan over a low heat, or cook it in the top of a double boiler, stirring constantly until it is thick enough to coat the back of a wooden spoon. Remove the custard from the heat, cover, and set it aside to cool.

Freeze in an ice cream maker, following the manufacturer's instructions. Or still-freeze (page 8), whisking the partially frozen ice at least once during the freezing process.

Toasted nuts and brittle caramel ground together to a fine powder are an indispensable flavoring for confectionery, perennially popular in chocolates, pâtisserie, and ices. Almonds and hazelnuts are the best nuts for praline.

SERVES 6

2oz/55g blanched almonds
4 egg yolks
8oz/225g caster sugar
¾ pint/425ml milk
¼ pint/150ml whipping cream, chilled

Heat the oven to 325ºF/160ºC/gas 3 and toast the almonds for about 10 minutes or until they are lightly browned. Spread them on a lightly oiled, heatproof surface.

Make the custard as described on page 37, using the egg yolks, 6oz/175gof the sugar and the milk.

Heat the remaining sugar with 4 tablespoons of water in a small, heavy pan until it dissolves, then boil to a deep golden brown. Pour immediately over the nuts—it does not matter if it does not cover them all—and leave until cold before crushing to a fine powder in an electric coffee grinder or with a pestle and mortar.

Stir the praline powder into the cold custard. Whip the cream until it holds soft peaks and fold it in.

Freeze in an ice cream maker, following the manufacturer's instructions. Or still-freeze (page 8), whisking the partially frozen ice at least once during the freezing process.

The flavorings of this ice are Indian, but its creamy texture is decidedly more European. Scandinavians use cardamom extensively in their baking and can buy the ground spice easily. To grind the whole spice, remove the aromatic seeds from their surrounding pods and crush them with a little sugar with a pestle and mortar. For a real Indian touch, decorate each serving with edible silver leaf, found in Indian shops. This is real silver beaten out as thinly as tissue paper.

SERVES 6

4oz/120g granulated sugar
¾ pint/425ml evaporated milk
about ¼ teaspoon ground cardamom
2oz/55g shelled pistachio nuts, chopped
¼ pint/150ml whipping cream

Add the sugar to 4 fl oz/125ml water in a heavy pan and heat gently until the sugar has dissolved completely. Raise the heat and boil the syrup for 5 minutes. Set it aside to cool, then stir in the evaporated milk, cardamom, pistachio nuts, and cream.

Freeze in an ice cream maker, following the manufacturer's instructions. Or still-freeze (page 8), whisking the partially frozen ice at least once during the freezing process.

This recipe uses good-quality dark chocolate (70 percent or more cocoa solids) and avoids an oversweet or overrich mixture, which would mask the chocolate flavor. Numerous variations on the basic formula are successful. To add a true orange flavor, rub the skin of an unwaxed organic orange with half a dozen sugar cubes and dissolve them in the hot custard. Or combine the partially frozen ice with lightly toasted, cooled, flaked almonds.

SERVES 6

6 egg yolks
4oz/120g caster sugar
½ pint/300ml milk
½ pint/300ml single cream
8oz/225g dark chocolate, grated
vanilla extract, to taste

Combine the egg yolks and sugar in a bowl. Whisk until the mixture is very pale and falls back leaving a trail when the beaters are lifted. Whisk in the milk, followed by the cream.

Cook the custard carefully in a heavy pan over a low heat, or cook it in the top of a double boiler, stirring constantly until it is thick enough to coat the back of a wooden spoon. Remove it from the heat. Stir the chocolate into the hot custard, then add a few drops of vanilla extract. Cover and set the custard aside to cool.

Freeze in an ice cream maker, following the manufacturer's instructions. Or still-freeze (page 8), whisking the partially frozen ice at least once during the freezing process.

Photograph on pages 34–35

CARDAMOM & PISTACHIO ICE CREAM

Butter and soft brown sugar cooked together until the sugar begins to caramelize give a rich butterscotch flavor to this unusual ice.
SERVES 6

3oz/85g butter
8oz/225g soft, light brown sugar
1¼ pints/750ml hot milk
4 egg yolks, beaten

Melt the butter in a heavy pan and stir in the sugar. Cook the mixture slowly until the sugar begins to caramelize, watching it very carefully so that it does not become too dark. Remove from the heat, stir in the hot milk, and continue stirring until the toffee has dissolved completely.

Allow the flavored milk to cool a little, then gradually stir it into the egg yolks. Strain the mixture back into the pan and cook it carefully over a low heat, or cook it in the top of a double boiler, stirring constantly until the custard is thick enough to coat the back of a wooden spoon. Remove the custard from the heat, cover, and set it aside to cool.

Freeze in an ice cream maker following the manufacturer's instructions. Or still-freeze (page 8), whisking the partially frozen ice at least once during the freezing process.

Photograph on page 84

BUTTERSCOTCH ICE CREAM

CARAMEL SORBET

This must be the simplest sorbet of all—just sugar, water, and a drop of lemon juice.
SERVES 6

12oz/350g granulated sugar
juice of 1 lemon

Pour ¼ pint/150ml of water into a heavy pan. Add the sugar and heat gently until it has dissolved completely. Wash down any sugar crystals from the sides of the pan with a pastry brush that has been dipped in cold water.

Raise the heat and boil the syrup to a light caramel, no darker than a rich golden brown or the sorbet will be bitter instead of sweet. Immediately remove the saucepan from the heat and dip its base into cold water to stop the sugar from darkening still further.

Add another 1 pint/600ml of water to the caramel and leave it to dissolve and cool, stirring from time to time to hasten the process. When the syrup is quite cold, stir in the lemon juice.

Freeze in an ice cream maker, following the manufacturer's instructions. Or still-freeze (page 8), whisking the partially frozen ice at least once during the freezing process.

Ices made with toasted brown breadcrumbs have been popular since the latter half of the eighteenth century. In nineteenth-century England, people decorated this ice with crystallized violets (page 93). Fresh raspberries are good too. Ideally, use organic brown bread for this recipe.

SERVES 6

3oz/85g fine brown breadcrumbs
3oz/85g granulated sugar
¾ pint/425ml double cream, chilled
2oz/55g icing sugar, sifted
2 tablespoons dark rum
real vanilla extract, to taste

Spread the crumbs on a baking tray and toast slowly under a grill, stirring from time to time, until an even golden brown. Be careful not to burn them. Set them aside to cool.

Add the sugar to 4 tablespoons of water in a pan and heat gently until the sugar has dissolved completely. Wash down any crystals from the sides of the pan with a pastry brush dipped in cold water. Raise the heat and boil the syrup to a rich brown caramel. Do not allow the caramel to darken too much or it will be bitter. Take it off the heat and stir in the crumbs.

Immediately turn the mixture on to a buttered baking tray. It will harden quickly into a kind of praline. Grind it finely in a coffee grinder or with a pestle and mortar. Do not try to grind this very hard mixture in a food processor or blender. It may damage the blades.

Whip the cream until it holds soft peaks, then beat in the icing sugar, rum, and a little vanilla extract. Fold in the sugared crumbs and still-freeze (page 8), without stirring.

Freshly roasted and ground coffee, especially if it is a high or dark roast, makes a superb flavoring for ices. Instant coffee can be used instead, of course, but the ice will have less distinction.

SERVES 6

4 tablespoons finely ground, fresh coffee
6 egg yolks
8oz/225g soft, light brown sugar
1 pint/600ml milk

Make fresh filter coffee with 6fl oz/175ml of boiling water, or pour the water onto the coffee in a jug, leave to infuse for a few minutes, then strain.

Combine the egg yolks and sugar in a bowl. Whisk until the mixture is very pale and falls back leaving a trail when the beaters are lifted. Whisk in the coffee and the milk.

Cook the custard carefully in a heavy pan over a low heat, or cook it in the top of a double boiler, stirring constantly until it is thick enough to coat the back of a wooden spoon. Take the custard off the heat, cover, and set it aside to cool.

Freeze in an ice cream maker, following the manufacturer's instructions. Or still-freeze (page 8), whisking the partially frozen ice at least once during the freezing process.

Ripe fruit is the secret of great fruit ices. Ripeness is the plant kingdom's strategy for reproduction, when optimum scent, sweetness, and lusciousness have maximum appeal to the creatures that will spread its seeds. Then, having ripened, most fruits deteriorate very fast, which is why so many today are sold while still unripe. They look good, but few will ever ripen properly to reach their full flavor. So when the garden produces a glut of berries, or a spell of good weather fills the market with perfumed heaps of strawberries and peaches, there is no better way to prolong the delicious moment than by making extravagantly juicy ices based on your FRUIT BOWL

For flavor, greengages and damsons are the aristocrats of the plum family, and both make excellent ices. Greengage ice cream is smooth, rich, and assertively flavored.

SERVES 6

1lb/450g greengages
4oz/120g soft, light brown sugar
4 egg yolks
4oz/120g icing sugar
½ pint/300ml double cream, chilled

Add ½ pint/300ml water to the greengages and brown sugar in a pan and bring to the boil. Cover and simmer the fruit until it is tender. This will take about 10 minutes, depending on the ripeness of the greengages.

Press the stewed fruit through a sieve. Discard the stones and chill the purée.

In a bowl set over a pan of simmering water, beat the egg yolks with the icing sugar until the mixture has tripled its original volume, then chill it.

Whip the cream with 2 tablespoons of iced water until it holds soft peaks. Combine the greengage purée, egg mixture, and whipped cream and whisk them lightly together.

Freeze in an ice cream maker, following the manufacturer's instructions. Or still-freeze (page 8), whisking the partially frozen ice at least once during the freezing process.

A really ripe melon, one that is so heavily perfumed that its character is plain, will make a memorable ice cream.

SERVES 6

1 ripe melon (about 1lb/450g)
juice of 1 lemon
6oz/175g soft, light brown sugar
½ pint/300ml whipping cream, chilled
2oz/55g crystallized ginger, finely chopped

Halve the melon, discard the seeds and spoon out the flesh. Purée it by pressing it through a sieve, or by processing it in a blender or food processor and straining it. Add the lemon juice and sugar to the purée and chill the mixture for about 2 hours, stirring it from time to time until the sugar has dissolved completely.

Whip the cream until it holds soft peaks, then combine it with the melon purée and the ginger.

Freeze in an ice cream maker, following the manufacturer's instructions. Or still-freeze (page 8), whisking the partially frozen ice at least once during the freezing process.

GREENGAGE ICE CREAM

STRAWBERRY ICE CREAM

Ripe, flavorsome fruit is essential to strawberry ice cream, but as long as damaged parts of the berries are discarded, there is no better use for less than perfect specimens. The orange and lemon juices help to bring out the flavor of the strawberries. The same technique and recipe are also suitable for raspberries.

SERVES 6

12oz/350g ripe strawberries, hulled
juice of 1 orange
juice of 1 lemon
6oz/175g caster sugar
¾ pint/425ml whipping cream, chilled

Juice the berries in an electric juicer or process them briefly in a blender or food processor and strain the purée. Alternatively, rub the berries through a sieve.

Combine the purée with the lemon and orange juices and sugar. Set the mixture aside for about 2 hours, stirring it from time to time until the sugar has dissolved completely.

Whip the cream until it holds soft peaks, combine it with the sweetened purée, and whisk them lightly together.

Freeze in an ice cream maker, following the manufacturer's instructions. Or still-freeze (page 8), whisking the partially frozen ice at least once during the freezing process.

Fully ripe mangoes are heavily perfumed, sumptuously flavored, and quickly made into a rich ice cream. Perfectly ripe peaches and nectarines can also be used.

SERVES 6

2 large ripe mangoes (about 1lb/450g)
juice of 1 lime or lemon
2oz/55g icing sugar
½ pint/300ml whipping cream, chilled

Peel the mangoes and cut the flesh from the stones. Purée the flesh with the lime or lemon juice either by processing it lightly in a blender or food processor, or by passing it through a sieve. Stir in the icing sugar.

Whip the cream until it holds soft peaks. Whisk the purée lightly into the cream.

Freeze in an ice cream maker, following the manufacturer's instructions. Or still-freeze (page 8), whisking the partially frozen ice at least once during the freezing process.

Photograph on page 96

The sweet flavor of soft fruits such as red currants and blackcurrants is improved by gently heating the fruit to extract the juice.

SERVES 6

1½ lb/700g redcurrants
8oz/225g caster sugar

Heat the oven to 350°F/180°C/gas 4.

Wash the red currants (there is no need to top and tail them) and shake off the excess water. Put them in a deep ovenproof dish with the sugar. Cover and bake for 30–45 minutes, or until the juices have run and the fruit is tender.

Pass the cooked red currants through a fine sieve to remove the skins, pips, and stalks. Leave the juice to cool completely.

Freeze in an ice cream maker, following the manufacturer's instructions. Or still-freeze (page 8), whisking the partially frozen ice at least once during the freezing process.

Raspberries need no cooking to turn them into fresh-tasting sorbets. Both fresh and frozen berries are suitable for ices. This recipe can be used for a variety of other intensely flavored soft fruits, including ripe strawberries, loganberries and mangoes.

SERVES 6

1lb/500g ripe raspberries
12fl oz/350ml basic sorbet syrup (page 88)
juice of 1 orange, strained

Rub the raspberries through a fine sieve to remove the pips, or process the berries briefly in a blender or food processor and strain the purée.

Combine the purée with the syrup and orange juice. If you have time, chill the purée for 1–2 hours in the refrigerator to allow the flavor to develop before freezing it.

Freeze in an ice cream maker, following the manufacturer's instructions. Or still-freeze (page 8), whisking the partially frozen ice at least once during the freezing process.

REDCURRANT SORBET

PASSION FRUIT PARFAIT

Passion fruit have a strong flavor and perfume that can stand dilution with eggs and cream. The ripe fruit look most unpromising, but until the skins are withered they will be less than their best. To extract the flesh, open passion fruit like boiled eggs and spoon out the seedy interiors. Freeze the parfait in individual glasses, or in a decorative ice cream mold.

SERVES 6

4 ripe passion fruit
8oz/225g granulated sugar
4 egg yolks
2 egg whites
8fl oz/225ml whipping cream, chilled

Open the passion fruit and sieve the flesh to extract the seeds. The amount of juice left to flavor the parfait will be small, but powerful.

Add the sugar to 6 tablespoons of water in a small, heavy pan and heat gently, stirring until the sugar has dissolved completely. Wash down any crystals from the sides of the pan with a pastry brush dipped in cold water. Raise the heat and boil the syrup until it is just beginning to color (about 300°F/150°C on a sugar thermometer).

Take the pan off the heat and set it aside to cool for 1 minute. While it is cooling, put the egg yolks into a large bowl and whisk them to a froth. Gradually whisk in the hot syrup, and continue whisking until the mixture is cool and has tripled its original volume. Whisk in the strained passion fruit juice, then chill the mixture.

Whisk the egg whites until they hold stiff peaks. Whip the cream until it holds soft peaks. Combine the yolk mixture with the whisked egg whites and cream, and whisk them together lightly.

Turn the parfait into freezer-proof individual dishes or into a single mold and freeze until firm. Serve on its own or with a soft fruit coulis (page 89), such as mango.

If the strawberries are perfectly ripe and soft enough to crush with your tongue against the roof of your mouth, then they can be puréed, sweetened, and frozen without much more ado. But if they are too firm to make a smooth purée without a fight, (and supermarket strawberries are bred to travel well), it is worth heating them to soften the flesh and extract more flavor. Serve strawberry sorbet on its own, with fresh strawberries or a mixture of soft fruits, or as an alternative to cream to accompany any pastry or meringue and soft fruit confection.

SERVES 6

1lb/450g ripe strawberries
freshly squeezed juice of 1 orange
8oz/225g caster sugar

Hull the strawberries carefully, removing any tough green or white parts at the stem end.

To use the uncooked method, purée the berries by pressing them through a sieve, or by processing briefly in a blender or food processor, and straining the purée. Stir in the orange juice and sugar, mix well, and set aside for an hour or two to let the flavor develop before freezing.

Use the cooked method for firmer berries. Roughly chop the strawberries and put them in a heavy-based, stainless steel pan with the orange juice and sugar. Cover and put on a very low heat for about 20 minutes, stirring occasionally, until the fruit has given up its juice. Purée the fruit by pressing it through a sieve, or by processing and straining the purée. Allow to cool completely before freezing.

Freeze in an ice cream maker, following the manufacturer's instructions. Or still-freeze (page 8), whisking the partially frozen ice at least once during the freezing process.

STRAWBERRY SORBET

RHUBARB SORBET

Forced spring rhubarb first appears in the depths of winter and makes an unusual pale pink ice. The flavor is perfectly captured by baking the rhubarb with sugar in a covered dish, without any added liquid.

SERVES 6

1½lb/700g spring rhubarb
10oz/280g caster sugar

Heat the oven to 350°F/180°C/gas 4.

Chop the rhubarb into short lengths and put it into a deep ovenproof dish with the sugar. Cover and bake for 45 minutes or until the rhubarb is very tender. Set it aside to cool.

Blend or process the fruit with its juice, or press it through a fine sieve to make a smooth purée.

Freeze in an ice cream maker, following the manufacturer's instructions. Or still-freeze (page 8), whisking the partially frozen ice at least once during the freezing process.

Capture the inimitable flavor of marmalade oranges during their brief winter season in this distinctive bitter orange sorbet. Use the same recipe for the other sour citrus fruits—limes, lemons, and grapefruit. Since their peel is invariably eaten, Seville oranges are not treated with fungicidal wax. This means that they do not keep as well as treated citrus fruits and should be used as soon as possible.

SERVES 6

1lb/450g Seville oranges
8oz/225g granulated sugar

Cut the zest from the oranges, using a very sharp knife or vegetable peeler, taking care not to include any of the pith.

Pour ¾ pint/425ml water into a pan and add the sugar and zest. Heat gently until the sugar has dissolved completely. Raise the heat and boil the syrup for 5 minutes, then set it aside until it has cooled completely.

Squeeze the juice from the oranges and strain it. Strain the cooled syrup, discarding the zest, then stir it into the orange juice.

Freeze the sorbet in an ice cream maker, following the manufacturer's instructions. Or still-freeze (page 8), whisking the partially frozen ice at least once during the freezing process.

Photograph on pages 46–47

Variation

Flavor the syrup with cardamom or coriander. Add 6 lightly crushed cardamom pods, or 1 tablespoon toasted and coarsely crushed coriander seed with the orange zest and sugar when making the syrup. Strain out the spices with the zest.

Create glorious homemade ice creams in just the time it takes to flavor a carton of cream or custard with fruit or a jar of something delicious from the store-cupboard and freeze it. Only a few of these ice creams need churning while they freeze, so they do tend to be rich. It is the generous amounts of cream and sugar that inhibit the formation of chunky ice crystals and allow these mixtures to freeze successfully without constant beating. Grating the zest of a lemon or peeling and mashing a banana are the toughest jobs demanded by these absurdly easy recipes for INSTANT ICES

MARMALADE ICE CREAM

Use the deep, dark taste of good marmalade to flavor ices, with or without the peel.

SERVES 6

½ pint/300ml marmalade
½ pint/300ml whipping cream, chilled
½ pint/300ml custard

Heat the marmalade and sieve out the peel. Cool the jammy part and the peel separately. Cut the peel into small pieces, if using.

Whip the cream until it holds soft peaks. Combine the jammy part of the marmalade together with the cream and the custard, and whisk lightly together.

Freeze in an ice cream maker, following the manufacturer's instructions, and stirring in the chopped peel, if using, before transferring the freshly churned ice cream to a storage box. Or still-freeze (page 8), whisking the partially frozen ice at least once during the freezing process and stirring in the chopped peel, if using, before freezing until firm.

A little of this rich banana ice cream goes a long way. Try it with a wedge of fresh pineapple.

SERVES 6

1lb/450g ripe, peeled bananas
4oz/120g icing sugar
juice of 1 orange
3 tablespoons dark rum
½ pint/300ml double cream, chilled

Mash or process the peeled bananas with the icing sugar, orange juice, and rum. Whip the cream until it holds soft peaks. Fold the banana purée into the cream.

Turn the mixture into a shallow freezer tray or freezer-proof individual serving dishes. Cover and still-freeze (page 8), without stirring, until firm.

Candied rose petals and rosewater perfume this pretty ice. The strengths of rosewaters vary, so add it a little at a time and taste. It will look the part, too, if decorated with whole crystallized rose petals (page 93).

SERVES 6

2oz/55g candied rose petals
4oz/120g icing sugar
¾ pint/425ml double cream, chilled
rosewater, to taste

Crush the candied rose petals almost to a powder. Combine the icing sugar with the cream and whisk until the mixture holds soft peaks. Fold in the candied rose petals and add rosewater a little at a time, bearing in mind that freezing will dull the flavor.

Turn the mixture into a shallow freezer tray or individual serving dishes, and still-freeze (page 8), without stirring, until firm.

ROSE PETAL ICE CREAM

HONEY ICE CREAM WITH LAVENDER

Lavender flowers are commonly used as a herb in the south of France, and pungent, lavender-perfumed honey is sold from roadside stalls alongside purple-cushioned fields. Use single cream if freezing this recipe in an ice cream maker and simply stir it into the honey.

SERVES 6

1 tablespoon fresh or dried lavender flowers
4 tablespoons icing sugar
¾ pint/425ml whipping cream, chilled
4oz/120g lavender honey

Using a food processor or pestle and mortar, grind together the lavender flowers and icing sugar.

If the honey is thick, thin it down with a little of the cream. Whip the remaining cream until it holds soft peaks, then mix in the lavender, sugar, and honey.

Turn the mixture into a shallow freezer tray or freezer-proof individual serving dishes. Cover and still-freeze (page 8), without stirring, until firm.

ROSE PETAL ICE CREAM

RATAFIA ICE CREAM

Making ratafia cookies is an excellent way of using up spare egg whites. They are easy to make (page 90) and excellent in ice cream as well as with it. Alternatively, use bought ratafia cookies or amaretti, and if there is a bottle of amaretto liqueur handy, a splash of it goes down well in or over the ice. Ratafia ice cream goes particularly well with a soft fruit coulis, such as raspberry or peach.

SERVES 6

4oz/120g ratafia cookies (page 90)
¾ pint/425ml whipping cream, chilled
4oz/120g icing sugar
almond extract, to taste

Crush the ratafias to coarse crumbs. Whip the cream with the icing sugar and a little almond extract until it holds soft peaks. Fold in the crushed ratafias.

Turn the mixture into a shallow freezer tray or freezer-proof individual serving dishes. Cover and still-freeze (page 8), without stirring, until firm.

Condensed milk provides the sweetening in this very easily made ice cream, which is so rich it needs no stirring while it freezes. A little of this ice goes a long way, so serve it in small scoops, or accompanied by a contrasting tart fruit sauce or sorbet.

SERVES 6

½ pint/300ml double cream, chilled
6fl oz/175ml sweetened condensed milk, chilled
vanilla extract, to taste

Pour the cream and condensed milk into a bowl, add vanilla extract to taste, and whip until the mixture holds soft peaks. When adding the flavoring, remember that freezing will dull its intensity.

Turn the mixture into a shallow freezer tray, or into freezer-proof individual serving dishes. Cover and still-freeze (page 8), without stirring, until firm.

Variation

WHITE CHOCOLATE DREAM Flavor the whipped condensed milk and cream with chocolate extract to taste and 2oz/55g of grated white chocolate.

This lemon ice cream is quite simply sumptuous, as are all citrus fruit ice creams made using the same method. It may be frozen in individual serving containers—hollowed out lemons are pretty or used as a piped topping for more elaborate frozen desserts, or as a filling for the lemon meringue pie baked Alaska (page 73).

SERVES 6

3 juicy lemons, preferably unwaxed
6oz/175g icing sugar
¾ pint/425ml double cream, chilled

Using a fine grater, grate the zest from 2 of the lemons, and squeeze the juice from all 3. Combine the zest, juice, and sugar. Whip the cream with 3 tablespoons of iced water until it holds soft peaks, then whisk in the sweetened lemon juice.

Turn the mixture into a shallow freezer tray, or freezer-proof individual serving dishes. Cover and still-freeze (page 8), without stirring, until firm.

To make the lemon wedges photographed here, fill emptied half-shells. Freeze till firm and cut in two.

LEMON ICE CREAM

COCONUT & LIME SHERBET

Coconut milk now comes ready to use in cartons, sachets, and tins, which are much less work than cracking open fresh coconuts, shredding the flesh, and squeezing the juice. Marry the smoothness of coconut with the aromatic juice of fresh limes for an ice that has a breath of the South Seas.

SERVES 6

3 fresh limes, preferably unwaxed
6 cubes of white sugar
4oz/120g icing sugar
1 pint/600ml coconut milk

Wash the limes in warm water and then dry them. Rasp the lime zest with the sugar cubes to extract a little of the lime oil, then cut open the fruit and squeeze the juice. Strain the juice into a bowl and add the cube sugar and icing sugar. Stir until the sugar has dissolved completely, then mix in the coconut milk. Taste and add more sugar if the flavor of lime is too sharp, remembering that freezing dulls flavors.

Freeze in an ice cream maker, following the manufacturer's instructions. Or still-freeze (page 8), whisking the partially frozen ice at least once during the freezing process.

LEMON ICE CREAM

A tin of chestnut purée, sweetened and lightly flavored with vanilla, is a useful standby in any store-cupboard. As a variation on this easy ice cream, stir a handful of broken meringue into the ice when it is partially frozen, then freeze until firm. Or serve it sprinkled with grated chocolate. Use single cream if freezing this recipe in an ice cream maker.

SERVES 6

8oz/225g sweetened chestnut purée
2 tablespoons sweet sherry or milk
½ pint/300ml whipping cream, chilled
2oz/55g icing sugar

Combine the chestnut purée with the sherry or milk, and mix to a smooth paste.

Whip the cream with the icing sugar until it holds soft peaks, and fold it into the chestnut purée.

Turn the mixture into a shallow freezer tray or freezer-proof individual serving dishes. Cover and still-freeze (page 8), without stirring, until firm.

CHESTNUT ICE CREAM

CHAZEL ICE CREAM

Chocolate and hazelnuts taste marvelous together, as confectioners have long understood. Choose a good-quality chocolate and hazelnut spread of for this exceptionally easy ice cream.

SERVES 6

¾ pint/425ml whipping cream, chilled
4oz/120g chocolate and hazelnut spread
2oz/55g icing sugar

Stir about 6 tablespoons of the cream into the chocolate and hazelnut spread to slacken it. Whip the remaining cream with the icing sugar until it holds soft peaks. Fold the chocolate and hazelnut mixture into the cream.

Turn the mixture into a shallow freezer tray or individual serving dishes. Cover and still-freeze (page 8), without stirring, until firm.

Dulce de leche in Spanish, confiture de lait in French, and banoffee toffee in English, are all names for caramelized condensed milk, the world's most irresistible sweet milk preserve. Find it under any, or all, of these names alongside jams, marmalades, honeys, and peanut butter. Use it to flavor wickedly easy ices by mixing it with lightly whipped double cream or mascarpone, natural yogurt, or a carton of fresh custard.

SERVES 6

½ pint/300ml banoffee toffee
1 pint/600ml fresh custard

Whisk together the banoffee toffee and custard.

Freeze in an ice cream maker, following the manufacturer's instructions. Or still-freeze (page 8). The custard-based version will be the better for being whisked at least once during the freezing process. Richer versions made with double cream or mascarpone need no whisking at all.

Photograph on pages 58–59

Variations

Ring the changes with nuts—chopped pecans, toasted hazelnuts, and toasted flaked almonds—chips or flakes of white, milk, or dark chocolate, or crisp, crushed cookie crumbs.

An ice cream so easy that children can make it for themselves. Ring the changes with creamy fromage frais instead of half, or all, the cream.

SERVES 6

9oz/250g ripe, peeled bananas
juice of 1 lemon
5oz/150g banoffee toffee (above)
½ pint/300ml single cream

Mash the bananas and stir in the lemon juice, banoffee toffee, and cream, or blend them together in a food processor.

Freeze in an ice cream maker, following the manufacturer's instructions. Or still-freeze (page 8), whisking the partially frozen ice at least once during the freezing process.

Victorian and Edwardian chefs made astoundingly elaborate ice cream confections to delight the guests who dined at their masters' tables. Now, of course, most of us do our own cooking, and elaborately towering ice cream molds are more often found in antique shops than in our kitchens. These days, frozen desserts may be simpler, but their homemade goodness and prepared-in-advance ease ensure that they are a popular choice for fuss-free entertaining; so join in the revival of these **RETRO RECIPES**

LEMON MERINGUE PIE BAKED ALASKA

Taking still-frozen ice cream covered in a cloud of hot meringue out of the oven always elicits gasps of surprise. Lemon meringue pie baked Alaska is a dessert to delight children and adults alike for its good taste as well as its dramatic entrance.

SERVES 6–8

For the shortcake base
4oz/120g self-raising flour
1oz/25g ground almonds
a pinch of salt
finely grated zest of 1 lemon
2oz/55g caster sugar
5oz/150g butter
1 egg yolk
For the filling
1 recipe lemon ice cream (page 66)
For the topping
3 egg whites
3oz/85g caster sugar

Preheat the oven to 375°F/190°C/gas 5.

Mix together the flour, ground almonds, salt, lemon zest, and sugar. Rub in the butter by hand, or using a food processor, until the mixture resembles coarse breadcrumbs. Add the egg yolk and mix briefly. Press the mixture evenly over the base of a round, shallow, loose-bottomed 8in/20cm cake tin. Bake for about 20 minutes, until the shortcake is just beginning to shrink from the edge of the tin. Remove the outer ring of the tin, but not the base, and leave the shortcake to cool.

To freeze the lemon ice cream mixture, prepare a round, deep, loose-bottomed 6in/15cm cake tin by lining the base and sides with non-stick baking parchment. Turn the ice cream mixture into the prepared tin and freeze it until firm.

To assemble the baked Alaska, put the shortcake base on an ovenproof serving platter or a baking sheet. Remove the ice cream from its tin, peel off the papers, and position the ice cream on the shortcake base. Return this work-in-progress to the freezer.

Preheat the oven to 450°F/230°C/gas 8. Then 10–15 minutes before serving, make the meringue by whisking the eggs whites until they hold soft peaks, and whisk in the sugar, a little at a time, until the meringue is thick, glossy, and holds firm peaks.

Spoon or pipe the meringue in an even layer over the top and sides of the ice cream to meet the shortcake base, but leave it showing.

Bake for about 5 minutes to brown the top of the meringue a little. Serve at once.

This is a classic duo of pistachio ice cream and praline-flavored bombe mousse named by the great chef Escoffier, who invented an entire alphabet of luxurious bombe combinations. Make one big bombe, adjusting the quantities of ice cream and bombe mousse to fit the mold, allowing a total of about 1¾ pints/1 liter for 6 generous servings. Or, make individual bombes using coffee cups. The smaller the cups, the more numerous the servings.

SERVES 6

1 pint/600ml cardamom and pistachio
    ice cream (page 42)
1½oz/40g blanched almonds
1½oz/40g caster sugar
4fl oz/120ml double cream, chilled
½ pint/300ml basic bombe mousse (page 88)

Chill the bombe molds or coffee cups well in the freezer. Ripen the pistachio ice cream in the refrigerator (page 9) until it is soft enough to be spooned. Line the molds with pistachio ice cream, shaping it into an even layer right up to the rim. Cover and freeze until the ice cream is firm again.

Use the almonds and sugar to make praline, as described on page 41, and grind the praline finely. Whip the cream until it holds soft peaks, then combine with the bombe mousse and powdered praline.

Spoon or pipe this mixture into frozen pistachio ice-lined cups, overfilling the centers to finish with a cappuccino-head flourish. Cover and freeze until firm.

Ripen the bombes for 5–10 minutes in the refrigerator before serving with small, crisp cookies.

The final bombe in Escoffier's ice cream alphabet is lined with coffee ice cream and filled with orange curaçao-flavored mousse. Alternative orange-flavored liqueurs include Grand Marnier and Cointreau.

SERVES 6

1 pint/600ml coffee ice cream (page 45)
4fl oz/120ml double cream, chilled
3 tablespoons orange curaçao
½ pint/300ml basic bombe mousse (page 88)

Chill a bombe mold well in the freezer. Ripen the coffee ice cream (page 9) until it is soft enough to be spooned. Line the mold with a layer of coffee ice cream, keeping the thickness as even as possible right up to the rim. Cover and freeze until the ice cream is firm.

Whip the cream with the curaçao until it holds soft peaks, then whisk it lightly into the bombe mousse. Spoon into the lined bombe mold, filling it completely. Cover and freeze it until firm.

To serve the bombe, remove the cover and invert the mold onto a plate while it is still frozen hard. Wring out a cloth in hot water and use it to wrap around the mold. Then, holding the plate and mold together firmly, shake the bombe out of its container. Return the bombe to the freezer if not required immediately, or refrigerate it to ripen (page 9), after smoothing over the surface if necessary and mopping up any drips.

BOMBES ABOUKIR

ICED CARAMEL MOUSSE

Almond ratafia (page 90), amaretti, or chocolate cookies can be used to make the crumb covering of this frozen caramel mousse.

SERVES 6

8oz/225g sugar
juice of 1 lemon
1 tablespoon powdered gelatin
2 egg whites
a pinch of salt
½ pint/300ml double cream, chilled
4oz/120g cookie crumbs

Prepare a 2lb/900g loaf tin by lining it smoothly with baking parchment or foil.

Add the sugar to 6 tablespoons of water in a heavy pan and heat gently, stirring, until the sugar has dissolved completely. Wash down any crystals from the sides of the pan with a pastry brush dipped in cold water. Raise the heat and cook the sugar until it turns a rich golden brown. Watch it carefully because if it darkens too much, the caramel will be bitter.

As soon as the caramel is sufficiently colored, take the pan off the heat and immediately dip its base in cold water to stop the temperature rising further. Stir in ¼ pint/150ml of water. The caramel will set hard on contact with the water, but will soon melt again with an occasional stir. When completely dissolved it will be a rich, mahogany-colored syrup.

Pour the lemon juice into a small pan with 2 tablespoons of water and sprinkle the gelatin over it. Set it aside for a few minutes to let it swell and soften. Then heat very gently, without allowing it to boil, until the gelatin is completely melted. Stir the warm liquid gelatin into the caramel syrup and set it aside until it is cool and beginning to set.

Whisk the egg whites with a pinch of salt until they hold firm peaks. Whip the cream until it, too, holds firm peaks. Combine the caramel syrup with the whisked egg whites and cream and whisk them together lightly. Turn the mixture into the prepared loaf tin, level the surface, and freeze.

Remove the frozen mousse from the tin and strip off its lining papers. Allow the outside to soften a little, then press the cookie crumbs all over the surface. Return the dessert to the freezer until it is needed. If it is to be stored for more than an hour or two, it should be covered to prevent ice crystals from forming on it.

Very rich and dark, chocolate marquise is frozen in a brick-shaped loaf tin and sliced straight from the freezer. Serve a slice on a chilled plate that has been flooded with a layer of vanilla or coffee sauce—simply the custard bases of those ices (pages 37 and 45), before freezing. Additions to a basic marquise can include broken meringue or rum-soaked raisins.

SERVES 6

8oz/225g fine-quality dark chocolate
4oz/120g unsalted butter, diced
2 eggs, separated
a pinch of salt
3oz/85g icing sugar
For the decoration
dark-roast coffee beans

Grate or break the chocolate into a bowl and add the butter. Heat gently over a pan of simmering water, stirring occasionally until the mixture is smooth.

In a second bowl, whisk the egg whites with the salt until they hold stiff peaks.

In a third bowl, beat the egg yolks with the sugar until the mixture is pale and fluffy.

Mix the melted chocolate lightly into the yolk mixture, then fold in the whisked whites. Spoon the mixture into a non-stick 2lb/900g loaf tin, cover the top with foil, and freeze until firm.

To serve, turn the marquise onto a chilled serving plate. Decorate the top with a few glossy coffee beans.

CHOCOLATE MARQUISE

Lots of ice cream and not too much cake is the right formula for ice cream cakes. Rich ices that neither freeze too hard nor melt as soon as you look at them are the ones to choose for assemblies such as this.

SERVES 20

For the cake
4 eggs
4oz/120g caster sugar
3oz/85g plain flour
1oz/25g cocoa
1 teaspoon baking powder
1 x 12in/30cm meringue layer (page 92)

For the filling
1 recipe chocolate ice cream (page 42)
1 recipe chazel ice cream (page 68)
1 recipe chocolate marquise (opposite)

For the decoration
¼ pint/150ml sweetened condensed milk
4oz/120g dark chocolate, broken up
½ pint/300ml whipping cream, chilled

Heat the oven to 400°F/200°C/gas 6.

To make the cake, beat the eggs with the sugar until the mixture is pale and thick, and falls back leaving a trail when the beaters are lifted. Sift together the flour, cocoa, and baking powder, and fold them into the egg mixture. Turn into a 12in/30cm round, spring-form cake tin lined with baking parchment and bake for about 15 minutes or until a skewer inserted into the center comes out clean.

Leave the cake to cool in its tin for 10 minutes before turning it onto a wire rack and stripping off the lining paper. When it is quite cold, split it into 3 layers.

To assemble the ice cream cake, put the first sponge layer on a flat serving plate or base, checking first that the freezer door will shut behind it. Spread the cake with the chazel ice cream which has been partially frozen, or if made earlier, ripened to a spreadable consistency (page 9). Top with the meringue and freeze until firm.

Spread the partially frozen or softened chocolate marquise over the meringue and top with the second sponge layer. Freeze until firm.

Spread a layer of partially frozen or ripened chocolate ice cream over the sponge and top with the last sponge layer. Freeze until firm.

To make the frosting, heat the condensed milk and chocolate in a pan, stirring until the chocolate has melted. Allow to cool, then chill in the refrigerator.

Whisk the chilled chocolate mixture vigorously to lighten it. Whip the cream until it holds soft peaks, then combine it with the chocolate mixture, whisking them together lightly.

Spread the top and sides of the cake with the chocolate cream. This can be finished in one of two ways: either pull it into frosted peaks using the tip of a rounded knife; or smooth it completely and comb it with wavy lines, using a clean, coarse-toothed comb.

Freeze the cake just long enough to firm the frosting, then cover it and freeze till firm.

Iced soufflés are every bit as dramatic as the hot kind and involve no strain on the cook's nervous system. An iced soufflé cannot flop. Raspberries are ideal for this type of soufflé because their intense flavor survives dispersal through a cloud of whipped cream and meringue.

SERVES 6

12oz/350g ripe raspberries, fresh or frozen
    and thawed
4 oz/120g caster sugar
2 tablespoons orange liqueur, or fresh
    orange juice
2 egg whites
2oz/55g icing sugar
¾ pint/450ml whipping cream, chilled

Wrap a strip of double-thickness baking parchment or oiled greaseproof paper round the outside of a straight-sided 1¾ pint/ 1 liter soufflé dish, or around 6 individual ramekins. The paper should come 1½in/4cm above the rim of the big dish (less for the individual dishes) to make a collar. Secure the join with a pin, and chill the dish or dishes.

Set aside a dozen perfect raspberries to decorate the finished soufflé. Purée the remaining raspberries either by pressing the fruit through a fine sieve to remove the pips, or by processing them briefly in a blender or food processor and straining the pulp. Stir in the caster sugar and orange liqueur (or juice). Set aside for at least 1 hour to allow the flavor to develop, stirring from time to time until the sugar has dissolved.

Whisk the egg whites until they hold soft peaks, then add the icing sugar and whisk until the mixture holds firm peaks. Whip the cream until it holds soft peaks.

Whisk the purée, whisked egg whites and cream together lightly, and immediately turn the mixture into the prepared dish or dishes. Smooth the top and cover with foil—keeping it away from the top of the soufflé—and freeze until firm.

Remove the foil and the paper collar before ripening the soufflé to serve it (page 9). Decorate the top with the reserved raspberries.

Photograph on pages 70–71

ICED RASPBERRY SOUFFLÉ

Real maple syrup tastes so much better than the cheaper synthetic kind that it is worth searching out. It keeps almost indefinitely, which is more than can be said of pecans, or any other nuts for that matter. Their oil gradually turns rancid during storage, so buy them fresh and use them quickly.

SERVES 6

1 tablespoon powdered gelatin
4fl oz/120ml maple syrup
3 eggs, separated
a pinch of salt
2oz/55g icing sugar
¾ pint/425ml double cream, chilled
2oz/55g shelled pecans, chopped
For the decoration
pecan halves

Wrap a strip of double-thickness baking parchment or oiled greaseproof paper around the outside of a straight-sided 1¾ pint/1 liter soufflé dish, or around 6 individual straight-sided ramekins. The paper should come 1½ in/4cm above the rim of the big dish (less for the individual dishes) to make a collar. Secure the join with a pin, and chill the dish or dishes.

Sprinkle the gelatin over 4 tablespoons of cold water in a small pan and set it aside for a few minutes until the gelatin has softened and swollen. Heat very gently, stirring, without allowing it to boil, until the gelatin has melted completely. Set aside.

Pour the maple syrup and egg yolks into a bowl over a pan of simmering water and whisk until the mixture is lukewarm. Take the bowl off the heat and continue whisking until the mixture is cool and has tripled its original volume.

In a second bowl, whisk the egg whites with a pinch of salt until they hold soft peaks, then add the icing sugar and whisk until the meringue holds stiff peaks.

In a third bowl, whip the cream until it holds soft peaks.

Combine the gelatin with the yolk mixture, whisked egg whites, and whipped cream, and whisk them together lightly. Fold in the chopped pecans and turn the mixture into the prepared dish or dishes. Cover with a lid of foil—keeping it away from the top of the soufflé—and freeze until firm.

Remove the foil and the paper collar before ripening the soufflé to serve it (page 9). Top with the pecan halves.

If you have time at the last minute, dip the decorative nuts in liquid caramel—4oz/120g sugar cooked with 4 tablespoons of water until golden brown—and set them on a greased surface to cool and harden.

Photograph on page 87

There is no branch of dessert making that offers more scope for personal

creation, or lends itself so easily to inspired invention than ice cream and

sorbet making. Topped with fruity coulis or hot chocolate sauce, and

accompanied by something crisp and dainty in the cookie line, desserts don't

get more irresistible than home-made ices. So for the foundations and

finishing touches of your creations, try these BASIC RECIPES

HOT CHOCOLATE FUDGE SAUCE
WITH BUTTERSCOTCH ICE CREAM

Sweetened condensed milk and plain chocolate combine in an easy-to-make and hard-to-resist hot fudgy sauce. The contrast of hot sauce on cold ice cream is a pleasure that cannot be improved upon.

MAKES ABOUT ½ PINT/300ML

2oz/55g dark chocolate
4fl oz/120ml sweetened condensed milk
4 tablespoons fresh milk
1oz/25g unsalted butter

Break the chocolate into a bowl or the top of a double boiler. Add the condensed milk and heat over simmering water, stirring until the chocolate has melted and the sauce is smooth. Beat in the milk, followed by the butter. Serve hot.

The combination of sugar and butter caramelized together and tempered with a pinch of salt adds up to the inimitable flavor of butterscotch.

MAKES ABOUT ½ PINT/300ML

3oz/85g butter
8oz/225g soft, brown sugar
¼ teaspoon salt
¼ pint/150ml double cream

Melt the butter in a heavy pan and stir in the sugar. Cook the mixture slowly until the sugar begins to caramelize, watching it very carefully to ensure that it does not become too dark. Remove from the heat and stir in 6 tablespoons of water. When the mixture is smooth, stir in the salt and cream.

Named after the curved, overlapping roof tiles of Provence, these crisp little cookies are shaped by being draped over a rolling pin while they are warm from the oven and still pliable. Alternatively, they can be rolled right round the handle of a wooden spoon to make cigarette cookies, or, of course, left flat. This classic, buttery recipe is great for using up egg whites left over after making custard-based ices.

MAKES ABOUT 50

4oz/120g butter, softened
4oz/120g caster sugar
5 large egg whites
real vanilla extract, to taste
4oz/120g plain flour

Heat the oven to 400°F/200°C/gas 6.

Cream the butter in a mixing bowl, add the sugar, and beat until the mixture is pale and fluffy. Beat in the egg whites, a little at a time, and a few drops of vanilla extract, then fold in the flour.

Pipe or spoon small mounds of the mixture onto well-greased baking sheets, spacing them well apart so that they have room to spread. Bake for about 10 minutes, or until they are pale gold in the center and darker at the edges.

Shape while still warm, then cool the tuiles on a wire rack. As soon as they are quite cold, store them in an airtight tin.

BUTTER TUILES

BRANDY SNAP BASKETS

Brandy snaps can be molded into baskets, making crisp containers for creamy ices. Bake the snaps a few at a time and mold them while they are still hot from the oven, over inverted cups or tumblers that have been well oiled or buttered. Leave to harden before removing.

MAKES ABOUT 6

2oz/55g butter
2oz/55g caster sugar
2 tablespoons golden syrup or molasses
2oz/55g plain flour
a pinch of salt
½ teaspoon ground ginger
1 teaspoon lemon juice
1 teaspoon brandy

Heat the oven to 325°F/160°C/gas 3 and line a baking sheet with baking parchment or buttered greaseproof paper.

Heat the butter, sugar, and syrup or molasses in a small pan until the mixture is warm and melted but not hot.

Sift together the flour, salt, and ginger and stir them into the liquid butter mixture. Stir in the brandy and lemon juice.

Drop 2 tablespoonful blobs of batter, 4 at a time, onto the prepared baking sheet, spacing them well apart. Bake for 8–10 minutes, or until they are brown and bubbling.

Remove from the oven and allow the brandy snaps to cool on the tray for about 1 minute before lifting them, one at a time, and draping them over well-oiled inverted cups or tumblers. As the cookies dry they become brittle and firm.

Photograph on pages 82–83

BUTTER TUILES WITH
ICED MAPLE PECAN SOUFFLÉ

A point to remember when constructing a bombe—usually in a tall metal dome, but a pudding basin does fine—is to put the softest ice in the center. This avoids a molten exterior with a rock-hard core. Parfaits (page 33) and many of the quick, still-frozen ices (pages 61–68) are suitable for bombe centers. Or there is the following basic bombe mousse, which can be flavored in numerous ways.

SERVES 6

4oz/120g granulated sugar
4 egg yolks
flavoring essence, to taste

Add the sugar to 4fl oz/120ml water in a pan and heat gently until the sugar has dissolved completely. Wash down any sugar crystals from the sides of the pan with a pastry brush dipped in cold water. Raise the heat and boil the syrup, not too briskly, for about 5 minutes.

Pour the egg yolks into a fairly large bowl and, whisking steadily, gradually add the syrup. Continue whisking until the mixture is thick and pale and about three times its original volume. Set the bowl in cold water, or over ice, and whisk until the mousse is cold.

Whisk in the flavoring. Cover and chill until needed. The mousse will keep for up to a week.

BASIC BOMBE MOUSSE

BASIC SORBET SYRUP

For almost-instant ices, basic sorbet syrup is a useful standby. It keeps for several weeks in the refrigerator, ready to combine at a moment's notice with fruit purée or juice and perhaps a liqueur.

MAKES ABOUT 3 PINTS/1.7 LITERS

1½lb/700g granulated sugar
1¾ pints/1 liter boiling water

Pour the boiling water over the sugar and stir until it has dissolved completely. Cool and store, covered, until needed.

Fresh sauces made with ripe, soft fruits complement many ices. Raspberry coulis is the chefs' favorite. Strawberry and mango are also especially good, but any other soft fruit, from peaches to kiwifruits, can be called upon.

Blackberries, blueberries and blackcurrants all make dramatically dark sauces, and the color and flavor of all three fruits are the better for being lightly cooked. In each case, sweat the fruit in a covered pan over a low heat until the juice begins to run, before puréeing it. Add just enough sugar to bring out the flavor of the fruit.

MAKES ABOUT 12FL OZ/350ML

1lb/450g ripe raspberries, fresh or
    frozen and thawed
about 4 tablespoons icing sugar
lemon juice, to taste

Purée the raspberries in an electric juicer, or by pressing them through a fine sieve, or by processing them briefly in a blender or food processor, then sieving them to remove the pips. Stir in the icing sugar and lemon juice to taste, then set the sauce aside for 1 hour, to allow the flavor to develop. Serve chilled.

Photograph on pages 82–83

Lighter and sweeter than plain whipped cream, a froth of Chantilly Cream is a classic topping. It can be flavored with a few drops of real vanilla extract, or a liqueur may be substituted for all or part of the water. Use as a topping on ices, coupes, or sundaes.

MAKES ABOUT 1 PINT/600ML

3 tablespoons water or liqueur
½ pint/300ml double cream, chilled
1 tablespoon caster sugar
real vanilla extract, to taste (optional)

Pour the water (or liqueur) into a bowl and chill in the freezer until ice crystals begin to form. Chill the beaters or whisk as well.

Add the cream to the bowl and whisk until the mixture holds soft peaks. Sprinkle on the sugar and a drop of vanilla, if used, and whisk in lightly.

Melting shortcake thins go well with any ice cream or sorbet. Stamp them out with plain or fancy cutters.

MAKES ABOUT 50

3oz/85g butter, softened
5oz/150g caster sugar
1 egg yolk
finely grated zest of 1 lemon (optional)
6oz/175g plain flour

Heat the oven to 350°F/180°C/gas 4.

Cream the butter in a mixing bowl, add the sugar, and beat until the mixture is pale and fluffy. Beat in the egg yolk, and lemon zest if used, then work in the flour and salt to make a stiff dough. Chill the dough in the refrigerator for about 30 minutes.

Roll out the dough to a thickness of about 5mm/¼in and stamp out the cookies, using a cup or glass if you don't have a set of cutters. Arrange them on greased and floured baking sheets and bake for about 10 minutes, or until pale gold.

Cool the cookies on a wire rack and, as soon as they are quite cold, store them in an airtight container.

Ratafia cookies, like tuiles, are useful for using up spare egg whites after making custard-based ices. These old-fashioned almond cookies can be served with ices, or crushed and incorporated into them.

MAKES ABOUT 100

5 egg whites
8oz/225g ground almonds
12oz/350g icing sugar
almond extract, to taste

Heat the oven to 300°F/150°C/gas 2.

Whisk the egg whites until they hold stiff peaks, then fold in the ground almonds, sugar, and extract to taste. Mix well to make a soft, sticky dough.

Pipe the mixture in small mounds (a teaspoonful or less) onto baking sheets lined with edible rice paper or non-stick baking parchment. Space the ratafias to allow for a little spreading.

Bake for about 45 minutes, or until the ratafias are quite dry and a pale, pinkish brown.

Leave the ratafias on the paper to cool on a wire rack. When they are quite cold, peel off the baking parchment, or trim the rice paper neatly around each ratafia.

Ratafias keep well for several weeks if stored in an airtight tin.

Brick pastry is used in North African cooking. The pale sheets look more like very thin pancakes than pastry dough. When painted with sweet melted butter and baked, half sheets make homemade cones that taste really good.

MAKES 20

3oz/85g caster sugar
2oz/55g butter
1 packet brick dough (usually 10 sheets)

Heat the oven to 350°F/180°C/gas 4.

Add the sugar to a small pan with 2 tablespoons of water and heat, stirring until the sugar has melted. Add the butter and stir until it too has melted.

Cut a circular sheet of brick dough into two halves. Brush one half with the sweet butter mixture, and shape it into a cone, butter side inside. Pin the cone in shape with a pin or toothpick, and set the cone, open end down, on a baking tray. Use the rest of butter and pastry to make 19 more cones.

Bake them for 10 minutes, or until lightly colored and crisp. Cool on a wire rack, and when completely cold, remove the pins or toothpicks and store the cones in an airtight container.

Photograph on pages 34–35

WAFERS Spread each sheet of brick dough very thinly with a scrape of the cookie mixture for making tuiles (page 86). Cut the sheets into sharp-edged shapes—squares, rectangles, diamonds or triangles—and lay them on a greased baking tray. Bake in a preheated oven 400°F/200°C/gas 6 for about 10 minutes. They will crisp as they cool on a wire rack.

For meringue nests, and for layers that can be built into all kinds of iced desserts, meringue made with hot sugar syrup gives better results than egg whites whisked with loose sugar. All types of meringue keep well once baked, but this one is quite stable before it is dried. It can be stored for several days in the refrigerator, and a spoonful or two used when needed to lighten a sorbet or whipped cream.

Copper bowls really do produce more and stronger meringue from fewer egg whites. The reason is a reaction between the metal and a component of egg. To maximize this effect, always use a balloon whisk with a copper bowl. When using an electric whisk, use a narrow, straight-sided bowl. Whichever method you use, make sure that the utensils are clean and dry, and that the egg whites are at room temperature.

MAKES 6 NESTS OR 2 X 9IN/23CM LAYERS

8oz/225g granulated sugar
4 egg whites

Pour ¼ pint/150ml of water into a small pan and add the sugar. Heat until the sugar has dissolved completely. Raise the heat and boil the syrup to the hard ball stage (about 250°F/120°C on a sugar thermometer). To test without a thermometer, drop a little of the syrup into iced water, then roll into a ball with your fingers. When the cold plunge firms the syrup sufficiently to roll it into a tough lump, it has reached the hard ball stage.

While the syrup is boiling, whisk the egg whites until they hold stiff peaks. Whisking continuously, gradually add the hot syrup. Continue whisking until the meringue is cold.

To make meringue nests, line one or more large baking sheets with baking parchment and mark on them 6 circles about 3½in/9cm in diameter.

Heat the oven to 225°F/110°C/gas ½.

Spoon large mounds of meringue onto the sheets, and use the back of the spoon to spread it into circles. Make a shallow depression on top of each mound.

Alternatively, fit a large piping bag with a plain nozzle at least ½in/1.5cm in diameter. Fill the bag with meringue and pipe circular bases, filling the outlines from the center outwards. Then pipe 2 neat circles, one on top of the other, around the edge of the bases.

Bake the meringue nests in the oven for about 3 hours. Check from time to time, and if the meringues begin to color, reduce the heat still further.

To make the meringue layers, mark prepared baking sheets with 2 large circles about 9in/23cm in diameter. Pipe a single layer of meringue, filling each circle from the center outwards. Alternatively, divide the meringue between the two outlines and spread it out evenly, using a spatula, to fill the circles.

Bake the layers at the same temperature as the nests.

MERINGUE

There is no comparison between the brash color and coarse texture of commercially crystallized flowers—usually violets and roses—and the delicacy of petals frosted at home. It is the simplest and most delightful of tasks, and once done, the flowers will last as long as a year. There are no prettier or more appropriate decorations for ices than fragile, scented, sugared flowers. Not all flowers are edible of course, but all in the following list are safe: primroses, violets, apple blossom, wallflowers, lavender, geraniums, pinks, carnations, roses, jasmine, lilac, borage, rosemary, thyme, and orange blossom. Check the safety of any flowers not listed. And the leaves of any of the culinary herbs, such as mint and rosemary, can be crystallized too, of course.

fresh, dry flowers in perfect condition—petals
    or small flowers
1 egg white
8oz/225g caster sugar

If you are crystallizing roses, or any other large flowers, separate them into petals. In the case of roses, nip off the white heel at the base of each petal. Very small flowers, individual lilac blossoms, violets, and primroses, can be left whole.

Break the egg white up a little with a fork in a saucer. Spread some of the sugar on a plate and put some more into a small sieve.

Using a small, soft brush, paint each petal or flower lightly all over with egg white. Lay the petals or flowers on the plate of sugar and sprinkle more sugar over them. The sugar sticks best to freshly painted petals, so coat and sugar them one at a time.

Lay the flowers on baking sheets lined with kitchen paper and dry them in a barely warm oven or the airing cupboard, for 24 hours or until they are dry and brittle. Turn the flowers several times in the first few hours of drying.

The color of the flowers is preserved remarkably well by this method. Once crystallized, flowers should be stored in airtight containers away from bright light.

INDEX

THIS PAGE: MANGO ICE CREAM, recipe on page 51
PAGE 4: LEMON VODKA SORBET, recipe on page 29

This revised and updated edition published in 2001 by
Conran Octopus Limited
a part of Octopus Publishing Group
2–4 Heron Quays, London E14 4JP
www.conran-octopus.co.uk

First published in 1986
Reprinted in 2004

British Library Cataloguing-in-Publication Data.

A catalogue record for this book is available from the British Library.

ISBN 1 84091 173 5

Publishing Director Lorraine Dickey
Senior Editor Muna Reyal

Creative Director Leslie Harrington
Senior Art Editor Carl Hodson
Photographer William Lingwood
Stylist Helen Trent
Food Stylist Lucy McKelvie

Production Director Zoe Fawcett
Production Controller Manjit Sihra

Thanks also to Hilaire Walden, Sunil Vijayakar for the food styling on p53, 72, 76, 82–3 and to The Conran Shop, Heals, Divertimenti, Purves and Purves for the loan of props.

Colour origination by Sang Choy International, Singapore

Printed in China